POISON DART FROGS

DOUG WECHSLER

THE ACADEMY OF NATURAL SCIENCES

The Rosen Publishing Group's
PowerKids Press™
New York

For Uncle Eddie, who appreciates frogs and nephews

About the Author
Wildlife biologist, ornithologist, and photographer Doug Wechsler has studied birds, snakes, frogs, and other wildlife around the world. Doug Wechsler works at The Academy of Natural Sciences of Philadelphia, a natural history museum. As part of his job, he travels to rain forests and remote parts of the world to take pictures of birds. He has taken part in expeditions to Ecuador, the Philippines, Borneo, Cuba, Cameroon, and many other countries.

Published in 2002 by The Rosen Publishing Group, Inc.
29 East 21st Street, New York, NY 10010

First Edition

Book Design: Emily Muschinske

Project Editor: Kathy Campbell

Photo Credits: All photos © Doug Wechsler.
pp. 4, 12, 16, 19 Strawberry poison dart frog (*Dendrobates pumilio*); p. 7 Granular poison dart frog (*Dendrobates granuliferus*); p. 7 Fire-bellied snake (*Liophis epinephalus*); pp. 8, 11 Black-legged poison dart frog (*Dendrobates bicolor*); p. 15 Rocket frog (*Colostethus talamancae*); p. 19 Blue poison dart frog (*Dendrobates azureus*); p. 20 Green and black poison dart frog (*Dendrobates auratus*); p. 20 Harlequin poison dart frog (*Dendrobates histrionicus*).

Thanks to Dr. Maureen Donnelly and Dr. Charles W. Myers for providing me with information about poison dart frogs.

Wechsler, Doug.
Poison dart frogs / Doug Wechsler.
   p. cm. — (Really wild life of frogs)
Includes bibliographical references (p.   ).
  ISBN 0-8239-5858-2 (lib. bdg.)
  1. Dendrobatidae—Juvenile literature. [1. Poison frogs. 2. Frogs.] I. Title.
  QL668.E233 W43 2002
  597.8'77—dc21
                                 2001000770

Manufactured in the United States of America

CONTENTS

A RAINBOW OF FROGS

You could paint a rainbow using the colors from the skin of poison dart frogs. In fact many of these little frogs look like they were painted by a mad artist. Poison dart frogs are among the brightest frogs in the world.

Colorful poison dart frogs have poisonous skin. Not all members of the poison dart frog **family** are brightly colored. About half of the **species** are mostly brown and blend in with the dead leaves on the ground. These brown species do not have poisonous skin. Poison dart frogs live in Central and South America. There are about 130 species in this family of frogs. Scientists are still discovering new species. They live mostly in rain forests in the lowlands and lower slopes of the mountains.

Strawberry poison dart frogs come in more colors than any other poison dart frog. Those living in Costa Rica are bright red.

SICKENING SKIN

Wild poison dart frogs make a variety of **toxins** in their skin. These **chemicals** protect them against animals that eat frogs, such as snakes, birds, and small mammals. The toxins also protect the frog's skin from **fungus** and **bacteria** that might cause disease. When a snake bites a poison dart frog, it soon lets go. Then it wipes its mouth against the ground. The poison might cause the snake to twist and turn for several hours before it recovers.

Most poison dart frogs are not dangerous to touch as long as you wash your hands carefully afterward. The golden poison dart frog should never be touched. The toxin can enter the **pores** in your skin. Licking your fingers after handling one of these frogs might kill you.

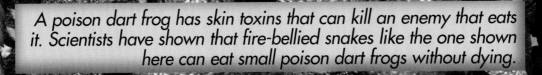

A poison dart frog has skin toxins that can kill an enemy that eats it. Scientists have shown that fire-bellied snakes like the one shown here can eat small poison dart frogs without dying.

DART POISON

Poison dart frogs got their name because some are used to poison blowgun darts. Only the Indians of the wet **Chocó** region of Colombia, South America, poison their darts this way. In other parts of South America, Indians use plant toxins on darts. The Chocó Indians use only three species of poison dart frogs.

The golden poison dart frog is so poisonous that the Indians only have to rub the dart tip against the skin of the frog. They are very careful to hold the frog with a leaf and not with bare hands. To get poison from the other two species, the Indians have to spear the frog with a sharp stick. This will make the frog release a lot of poison from the skin, but it will also kill the frog.

This black-legged poison dart frog from Colombia has strong toxins that the Chocó Indians use as poison for darts or arrows.

"DON'T EAT ME"

The bright colors of poison dart frogs send out a message to other animals, "Don't eat me." The colorful skin warns other animals that these frogs are dangerous to eat. The most common warning colors are yellow, orange, and red. These are often mixed with black. Many other animals, such as coral snakes, monarch butterflies, and milkweed beetles, wear these colors to send the same message to enemies.

The frog's warning colors and poison are good protection. Poison dart frogs can be seen in the open in the middle of the day when other frogs are hiding.

The bright colors of poison dart frogs, like the yellow of this black-legged poison dart frog, warn predators to stay away.

DOUG SAYS

SOME FROGS LOOK LIKE POISON DART FROGS TO FOOL THEIR ENEMIES INTO THINKING THEY ARE ALSO TOXIC.

DOUG SAYS

POISON DART FROGS LAY ONLY A FEW EGGS AT A TIME, USUALLY FROM 5 TO 20.

LOVE SONGS

The rain forest is a big place, so poison dart frogs need a way to find one another. The males call with whistles or **trills** to tell females where to find them. The calls also warn other males to stay away from the little patch of ground that is their place or **territory**.

When a female is ready to **mate**, she finds the calling male. While they mate, she lays eggs in a curled up leaf or other safe place. Poison dart frogs rarely lay eggs in water like many other frogs. Either the male or female will stay near the eggs until they hatch. Some poison dart frogs will urinate on the eggs to keep them moist.

Strawberry poison dart frogs like to call from leaves and twigs a few inches off the ground.

PIGGYBACK RIDES

It takes from 10 to 18 days for the tadpoles to form inside the eggs. When the eggs are ready to hatch, the parent backs up to the eggs. Once the tadpoles leave the eggs, they wriggle up their parent's back. A sticky slime on the parent's back keeps the tadpoles from falling off. Some poison dart frogs carry their tadpoles one at a time, while others carry them all at once. The parent hops with its tadpoles to the water. Some species bring the tadpoles to streams, some carry them to small pools, and others use water that gathers inside knotholes of trees.

The tadpoles take from 6 to 12 weeks before they turn into little frogs. The frogs then leave the water looking like tiny adults.

A poison dart parent carries its tadpoles on its back to water. This brown species, called rocket frog, is not poisonous.

TADPOLES IN A TINY POOL

Strawberry poison dart frogs and a few other species carry their tadpoles one at a time to a **bromeliad** plant. Bromeliads trap water at the base of each leaf. That water makes a tiny pool. The mother frog brings each tadpole to a different part of the plant so that it has its own pool. The tadpoles grow up in a pool that holds less water than a teacup. They share their home with mosquito **larvae** and other tiny creatures. Larger insects that eat tadpoles do not live in such tiny pools.

The mother strawberry poison dart frog feeds the tadpoles in a very unusual way. She lays eggs in the tiny pool. The tadpoles eat the eggs. This is the only food they eat until they become frogs.

Poison dart frogs are good climbers. When the tadpoles hatch, their mother carries them to the water-filled leaves of a bromeliad plant like the one shown here.

ANT PICNICS

Tiny frogs eat tiny **prey**. Ants are just the right size for poison dart frogs. Poison dart frogs eat more ants than any other food. Ants provide more than a good meal for these little frogs. The poisonous chemicals on the frogs' skin come from the ants. Other tiny animals are part of the poison dart frogs' diet. Mites, which are tiny relatives of spiders, are the second most important food. After that come beetles and springtails. Springtails are tiny jumping insects that live among the dead leaves on the ground.

Most frogs sit in a good spot and wait for a meal to come by. Poison dart frogs are always on the move. When they see a tiny insect, they lean toward it. They flick their sticky tongues out and pull it into their mouths.

Top: *A strawberry poison dart frog in a rain forest in Costa Rica looks for a meal.* Bottom: *The blue poison dart frog from Suriname is also an active hunter.*

CONSERVATION

The tropical forest homes of many poison dart frogs are in trouble. In many places, the forests have been cut to grow crops or raise cattle. When this happens, the frogs usually do not **survive**. Cutting the forests destroys the moist, shady places where poison dart frogs live.

Some kinds of poison dart frogs live in only one valley or on one mountaintop. If the forest in that valley or on that mountain were cut, then every frog of that species probably would die and the species would become **extinct**. Some species may have become extinct without ever having been seen by a scientist because so many tropical forests already have been cut.

Poison dart frogs need their homes in rain forests protected or they cannot stay alive.

AN ODDBALL POISON DART FROG

One member of the poison dart frog family stands out as being different from all the rest. The Venezuelan skunk frog seems to do everything opposite from all of its relatives. It is the only poison dart frog that is active at night. It is the only one that lives in water. It is twice as big as most members of the group. Females can grow up to 2 ½ inches (64 mm).

The Venezuelan skunk frog does not have poisonous skin. You can probably guess how it defends itself. When it is attacked or handled it gives off a skunklike odor. It is the only poison dart frog that smells bad.

GLOSSARY

bacteria (bak-TEER-ee-uh) Tiny living cells that are seen with a microscope.

bromeliad (bro-MEE-lee-ad) Plants in the pineapple family that store water at the base of their leaves.

chemicals (KEH-mih-kuls) Substances that can be mixed with other substances to cause reactions.

Chocó (choh-KOH) The very wet region of Colombia, South America, that is near the Pacific Ocean.

extinct (ek-STINKT) To no longer exist.

family (FAM-lee) The scientific name of a large group of plants or animals that are alike in some ways.

fungus (FUNG-ges) A mushroom, mold, mildew, or related organism.

larvae (LAHR-vee) The plural form of larva. The early life stage of certain animals that differs greatly from the adult stage.

mate (MAYT) When a male and female join together to make babies.

pores (PORZ) Tiny openings in the skin where oil is made.

prey (PRAY) An animal that is eaten by another animal for food.

species (SPEE-sheez) A single kind of plant or animal. For example, all people are one species.

survive (sur-VYV) To stay alive.

territory (TEHR-uh-tohr-ee) Land or space protected by an animal for its use.

toxins (TAHK-sinz) Poisons made by a plant or an animal that harm another plant or animal.

trills (TRILZ) Rapidly repeating musical notes.

INDEX

WEB SITES

To learn more about poison dart frogs, check out these Web sites:

http://daphne.palomar.edu/wayne/dartfrog.htm
http://library.thinkquest.org/C007974/2_2poi.htm?tqskip=1
www.aqua.org/animals/species/prpdfrog.html